Skunk Talk

Skunk Talk

Albert Garcia

BEAR STAR PRESS

For permissions and information, please contact
BEAR STAR PRESS
185 Hollow Oak Drive
Cohasset, California 95973
530.891.0360 / www.bearstarpress.com

Author photograph: Teresa Steinbach-Garcia
Cover art: Teresa Steinbach-Garcia
Book Design: Beth Spencer

ISBN: 0-9719607-7-1
Library of Congress Control Number: 2005926585

ACKNOWLEDGMENTS

The author thanks editors of the following publications and anthologies where these poems, sometimes in slightly different versions, first appeared:

Clackamas Literary Review: "Eeling, North of Tomales" and "Loquat"
Eclipse: "One Lesson"
The Hampden-Sydney Poetry Review: "Skunk Talk"
Mid-American Review: "The day I was born"
North American Review: "Waking"
Passages North: "What Do You Say, Grandfather?"
Poetry East: "August Morning"
Prairie Schooner: "I Watch You Paint"
Red Rock Review: "Ice" and "Cliff Jumping"
Reed: "Our Start," "Rain Gutters," and "Entering the Yard"
Southern Indiana Review: "Your Pregnancy"
Suisun Valley Review: "Late Autumn, Late Afternoon" and "Deer Creek Lodge"
Yankee: "Cooling"

"August Morning" also was published in the *Poetry East* anthology *Who Are the Rich and Where Do They Live?* "On Making Wood" appeared in *To Fathers: What I've Never Said* (Story Line Press), and "Frog Eggs" appeared in *Blue Arc West* from Tebot Bach.

for Terry, Anna, Michael, and Ben

Contents

Four

Five

August Morning

It's ripe, the melon
by our sink. Yellow,
bee-bitten, soft, it perfumes
the house too sweetly.
At five I wake, the air
mournful in its quiet.
My wife's eyes swim calmly
under their lids, her mouth and jaw
relaxed, different.
What is happening in the silence
of this house? Curtains
hang heavily from their rods.
Ficus leaves tremble
at my footsteps. Yet
the colors outside are perfect—
orange geranium, blue lobelia.
I wander from room to room
like a man in a museum:
wife, children, books, flowers,
melon. Such still air. Soon
the mid-morning breeze will float in
like tepid water, then hot.
How do I start this day,
I who am unsure
of how my life has happened
or how to proceed
amid this warm and steady sweetness?

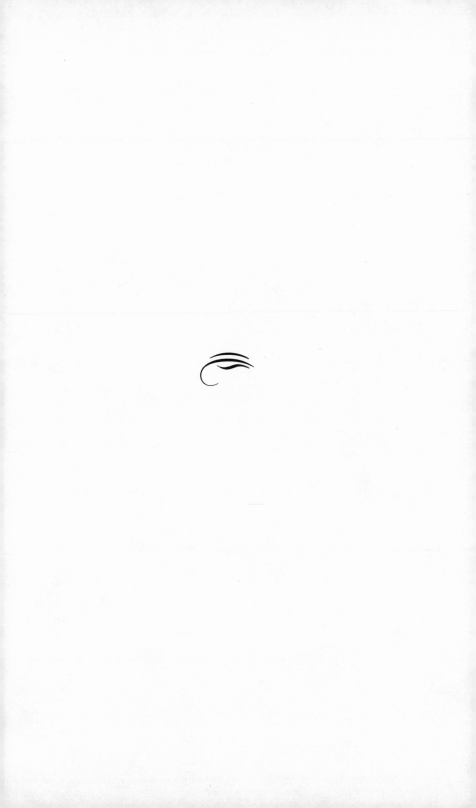

I Watch You Paint

After stretching
wet paper over board,
washing in
the first gray hues,
leaving white
where the man and woman
will stand,
you step back
and squint.

I like this,
watching you imagine,
seeing the picture
by looking at your eyes
and the muscles
of your face.
You mix another
layer of wash
and another, and soon
it's nearly complete
and I'm seeing it
as if with blurred eyes.

But you see more.
You're bleeding magenta
into the man's shirt.
The woman's black hair
crosses her face
and you scratch it
with a knife
for highlights.
Your brow creases.

I see now
the man's hand
is on her shoulder. There
is wind. Her white dress
blows tight against her body.
I want to ask you
what is happening
but it seems
the wind is in you.

And now what?
You've got a needle
to pick the dry pigment
from the man's eye,
leaving a tiny white dot
on his pupil
which, though small,
now makes me realize
he has the very expression
I sometimes get
when I'm angry.
You hate that look,
but there it is
in the man's eyes,
and now your brush
dashes around in his hair.

I haven't spoken
for hours.
The man clearly
is losing the woman.
You've washed
a darker gray
into the sky.

Finally, you sit back
and look across the room.
Then you glance at me,
and it seems
I haven't seen you in years.
I say the painting is sad.
You say
it's not finished.

Loquat

The shape your mouth makes
on the second syllable of *loquat*

is what happens after
you swallow the flesh

and hold the seed,
a slippery marble,

on your tongue. Never mind
that you haven't eaten one

in years, that you think this
when a woman

across from you at dinner
asks, *Your favorite fruit?*

The loquat
plops into your mind

and you say the word
not expecting

a sudden rush
of heat at your back

as if you're standing in July
under thick, leathery leaves—

a boy rolling a pit
between tongue and teeth—

a boy filling a pail
with dusty orange fruit.

You say the word *loquat*
and for moments after

feel a gush
of sugar at your throat.

'Possum

I hear scratching, open the kitchen door
to see short dense fur and pointed snout,
a 'possum, humble body and bare tail
on the top step. Small black eyes
peer up at me. He backs away, a gesture not of guilt
for eating cat food, nor fear, but slow
realization, instinct. Our obese cat
hisses at him, moans a threat
deep in her body as we watch him
amble across the concrete floor, past the lawnmower,
out into the black of night. It's cold,
frost coming, but inside minestrone bubbles on the stove.
My wife moves about the kitchen with floured hands,
yeast scenting the air. Our daughter finishes homework,
lessons about pioneers and gold,
sluice boxes, hydraulic mining, the damming
of California's streams. Her book lies open to a map—
the great Central Valley—blue veins of rivers
snaking their way to the delta. I'd like
to sit with this dark-eyed girl, talk
about the stories in her text. She gives me a look
that says she's been lectured to all day,
that her chapter is the voice of a very dull man,
that any word out of my mouth will be silt
swirled out of a miner's pan. So I say
I just saw a 'possum. In the garage—
a 'possum, but she's seen this fellow
before. Her back to me, my wife
stirs the soup on the stove. My daughter
stares down our dark hallway, past me,
memorizing the facts she'll need for tomorrow,
her mind flowing off to its own history.

ICE

In this California valley, ice on a puddle
is a novelty for children
who stand awkward in their jackets
waiting for the school bus.
They lift off thin slabs
to hold up in the early light
like pieces of stained glass.
They run around,
throw them at each other,
lick them, laughing as their pink tongues stick
to the cold, their breath fogging
the morning gray.
                    Between the Sierras
in the distance and a faint film
of clouds, the sun rises
red like the gills of a salmon.
From your porch, watching the kids,
you love this morning more
than any you remember. You hear
the bus rumbling down the road
like the future, hear the squealing
voices, feel your own blood warm
in your body as the kids sing
like winter herons, *Ice, ice, ice.*

Waking

He woke in the dark to feel
her changed. Her hip, the same
he'd let his fingers graze
each morning before sunrise,
felt cool, odd. Her hair—
what was it?—almost
like a doll's, not real.
He touched her shoulder, that round knob,
then reached for the nightstand lamp.
Her mouth, lips parted
nearly in a word, as if to say,
I'll be up, I'll get breakfast,
as she'd done for 40 years,
lay still, open. Under their lids
her eyes had receded. He felt
his own stubbled jaw,
then her cheek, her neck
under the flannel, traced
with his eyes her body's length,
the small mounds it made
in the quilt, then turned off
the lamp—carefully
placed his arm across her chest—
choosing to stay in bed
to wait for whatever would come
with morning's cold light.

The day I was born

the shad were running.
On a slow green stretch of river
a man hoisted three pounds
of flapping, mouth-gaping silver
onto hot smooth rocks
the way God, I imagine, lifted
me from nothingness
and plopped me gasping
into Enloe Hospital, Chico, California.
It was midmorning.
Walnut and almond orchards
steeped in the humidity
of valley irrigation.
Workers picked ripe apricots.

I want to say something extraordinary occurred—
a cure for a disease,
the discovery of a new species.
But I've researched the date: nothing happened.
I've even made up the part
about the shad fisherman
though it's likely
someone was out on the river
that same morning
feeling his line drift with the current,
content with a cold canteen of water
and the real possibility
of a catch, a story, something to add
to his drawn-out days of ordinary wonders.

Our Start

In this valley's fog, the sharp-shinned hawks
hunker on fence posts
beside the highway's damp asphalt,
fluff dark feathers off their bodies.

It's seven a.m. I steer
slowly, cutting low beams
through the veiled light. Between us,
on the seat: a jumble of maps, receipts, candy.

The mist, of course, will lift
in hours. Our road is quiet—my hands
grip the wheel. Your hair
gleams wet from the motel shower.

Deer Creek Lodge

The stream runs clear
but wire screens control
hundreds of trout
bumping head to tail—a line
of black backs all facing the current.

You can choose your dinner
from the little bridge.
Have the man dip his net
and carry your fish
fresh to the kitchen.

Enjoy this, your appetite
worked up by invigorating
pines and breeze. Yes,
feel good to stroll
by the deer in their cages.

Your son feeds a doe
from his hands.
She mouths the grass
with wet black lips, then nudges
her way along the chain mesh fence.

In the lodge, pine paneling tells you
you're in the right place.
You think of the doe's
big glossy eyes, her lashes
long, her face lonely, lovely.

The trout's flesh flakes
white on the plate in front of you,

tartar sauce in its pleated paper cup.
You feel the meat—
light, airy, mild—in your mouth.

You even savor steamed
green beans and parsley, marvel
at the photo of an osprey
in its pine-top nest.
As the sun bleeds down into trees

you think this is something
you can keep, this light
on the lacquered wood tables—
all despite the tightness in your lungs
when you walk in cooling air to the car.

Your Pregnancy

Glow, the word I think
as I pass my hand over
your stomach's tight skin,
the gloss of it. Seems
everything taking on new life
shines, and so stones
in the creek look
as if they might divide
or have been
while we weren't looking.

Eight months into this,
you're tired. I feel
guilt for my pleasure
in touching you. But it's a marvel,
this scene, this great swelling
hill, this waxy stretch
of possibility. Forgive me.
I am staring
because it is natural to gaze
at that which gives off light.

COOLING

If I closed my eyes
and focused on the gritty-smooth
pleasure of pear in my mouth
and listened to your voice
humming to our daughter,
your attempt to soothe her
into sleep—if I simply held
that pear flesh with my tongue,
letting it dissolve, savoring it
like a memory,
if your notes could linger
longer between these rooms—
if you would come in
after the child is asleep
and share with me
the last few bites
before we turn in, if you would
hum to me something old—
if I could keep this evening
in a drawer
that when opened would release
a breeze like the one outside, the one
that has been there all day
moving the curtains
but which is now finally cooling.

Upon Finding an Article on the Sea Cow

I could read all day
about the manatee
floating

amid mangroves, between
sea's brine and freshwater estuaries,
my thoughts

swimming sluggishly around
my living room's moist air,
bobbing

in and out of my mind
like the one-ton mammal
that eats

turtle grass and hyacinth to feed
her slow heart,
her coat

of fat covered by nearly-hairless skin
with white scars left
by boats'

propellers. Observe
her whiskered, kind face.
Observe

how she moves, her body
suspended in a dance so slow
it's easy

to believe the entire world
could be seduced by her grace
and think

as ancient sailors did
she's a mermaid, her wide
flat tail

moving the water behind her
with such power and beauty
that now

even in this room's still air
I've lost myself,
buoyant

as if a tide
surged and pressed at the walls,
washing

me along. I'm submerged
in these pages, sinking, floating
rising.

Framing

A breeze moves through the house.
Here are your fingers prying back
cardboard tabs that hold
the simple gold frame's small pane
of glass. Your fingers laying in
the photo of you, your smiling sister,
and a Jersey milk cow,
a picture that radiates her blonde hair
and that day's light
too brightly. Why
do you hang this on the hallway wall,
this reminder of a grief so intense
your red-knuckled hands
tremble sixty years later as you level,
amid portraits and wedding pictures,
the frame and its black and white image?

Can you still smell that morning—
lemon blossoms and dew and the earthy
musk of the Jersey—
just days before your sister fell ill,
a simple ear infection turned
to pneumonia? Do you still feel
the weight of the blue spring sky,
suddenly as immense as God,
a sky you looked to for comfort,
under which you found only yourself,
now the oldest, now the one daughter?
Do you even see yourself
in the picture, or is it all her,
the way a windy meadow
is all wind, pulling at you?

Skunk Talk

We're talking skunks. I say
I like the smell—not
the overbearing fog
left on a dog's snout,
but the gentle scent
they carry everywhere.

She says I'm nuts. They stink
plain and simple. She
wants more wine.
Sitting crosslegged
on the floor, she wants me
to get it. I ask

if she's ever felt the bottom
of their feet—patent leather.
I'm telling her
they make wonderful pets
if you find them young
and abandoned. Her face
is in a magazine,
fingers in her hair.

I pour more wine.
She won't look at me
and hums softly to herself.
I'm saying
all animals have odors—
it's a matter
of being used to them.

Then I'm thinking
of her hair, the way
she twirls it
in her left hand, its smell.
I used to bring it to my face
in the night

as she slept. I can't
recall the words
I would use to describe it.
Sweet? No. Fresh?
Wild? Let's go
to bed, I say.
She looks up
and moves her bangs from her eyes:
No more skunk talk?
No.

COHERENCE

In half-black of early morning, wind
from traffic stirs oleanders
in the freeway median.

My lips have left my daughter's
soft cheekbone, and now
they're in the warming air

of this car. Aware
of little, I chew an English muffin,
change lanes to get around

a cement truck. How I envy
the driver, who daily watches his gray soup
slide into forms,

smoothes it, knowing he'll make
something solid.
I'm on my way to a classroom

where I'll teach coherence. Sentences.
Paragraphs. That connecting to this.
Tomorrow, again, I'll drive

when the sky lightens
to a steel pink, the lines
of tail lights strung together

on a thread that could break
any second,
right in front of me.

Rain Gutters

She's on a ladder, scooping
decayed leaves and pine needles,
gravel washed off the asphalt shingles—
slopping the sludgy mess
into a paint bucket.

It's October, wood smoke
heavy in the air. The phone, snug
on its hook, is still warm
with my mother's news: gallstones,
stomach acid rising on its own.

Below, I'm feeding my wife
a hose to spray
the gutter's length,
waiting at the downspout
for the gush of black soup.

It's her silhouette
against the gray sky
that makes my hands release the hose
and brace the metal ladder
below her small cold feet.

What Do You Say, Grandfather?

for Carl Spanfelner

What do you think?
Roots upturned, grotesque
in the air, leaf mulch smell

lingering
but softened now
with dust.

What do you say
when 73 years
of orchard are gone?

Stand in the middle
of what the saws and dozers have done
and let your mouth go dry;

stick your hands in your pockets
or clasp them behind your neck.
Where you're standing

August sun is touching
for the first time
in six decades.

Don't look toward the house
alone now under the sky,
the windows

dark caves where nobody lives,
shrubs slowly winding
their way into the eaves.

Stare at the ground
where a few of last year's hulls
remain hot in the dirt.

Look at the bark wrinkling
over these toppled trunks,
and see the faces

of yourself
in different seasons—
pruning, harvesting,

grimacing
under the weight
of old mallets

you'd use to knock the limbs
until the air rained
walnuts. See your face

in the spring
as you walk the rows,
inspecting millions

of dangling catkins,
the caterpillar flowers you've seen
in your dreams.

See the sharp-edged faces
of your children
now working their own orchards,

their blood and breath intent—
as yours has been for years—
on the tired dry smell

of late September, when the first
flesh-colored bells
break wrinkled and hard from their skins.

See again the lay of this land,
gentle slope going down
to the river, obscured

for all these years by limbs
twisting through the sky; see
the same sweet loam

that drew you here
73 years ago,
a wiry young man who sensed

this was the place
his saplings would grow.
And they did.

July Evening

A breeze through the window screens—
we ate the salmon-fleshed crenshaw
she'd brought in from the field
and chilled since yesterday.

Across from each other, at the kitchen table,
we each scooped from our half melon
and let the fragrant juice
slosh around in our mouths.

We could have spoken
had there been anything to say.

Impressions

Come up our driveway and you'll curl around
to the side of our house, to the gaping
entrance of our garage.

Most people enter there, passing
the lawn mower, the washer/dryer,
the workbench covered by splattered paint

and cobwebs and old pieces
of sandpaper. That's where you'll encounter
the cat's bowl and the cat

spreading her ten-year-old, flabby, flea-powdered body
across the threshold to the kitchen.
That's where you'll see I've never finished

painting the doorframe (the caulking and primer
serving well enough), a daddy-longlegs
perched in permanent residence

in the corner. You'll have to step
over a tangle of children's muddy shoes
when you enter, and when you do

you'll see the glossy wood floor
and shining tile counters, photos
artfully arranged on the wall,

a bouquet of cosmos freshly centered
on the table. This is what
you were supposed to have seen first

had you taken the walkway around
the garage, past the planters
of pansies and Iceland poppies

and knocked on the front door.
There, through the ten-pane window,
you would have seen my face

smiling and freshly shaven
greeting you
in an entryway of bright and honest light.

A Scene: Driving Past the Corner Market

What did he say, this man
holding his infant daughter,

hovering over the flapping, spinning
pigeon, injured or poisoned, flailing

its dusty wings on the hot sidewalk
outside the corner market?

The moment it took me to drive past,
I could see his mouth

speaking to the baby. Was he explaining
this is what happens

when a bird glances into a car's fender,
when one grain of rat poison

looks like a bread crumb
and seizes a tiny nervous system?

Did he tell his daughter,
squirming in his arms to see

the bird's iridescent head,
green and purple, thrashing

from side to side, that this too
is nature, this spasmodic

preparation for death?
Was he thinking

he should step on the bird's head
to end the pain, to prevent

the girl, too young for words herself,
from seeing? Or was he saying

anything beyond, *Damn, look at that*,
amazed, on a warm spring day

on a walk to the market,
at the kind of frightening, beautiful miracle

the world can give a man
who holds tight to what he loves?

Fig

When we tear through its skin
it looks like flesh
with seeds

or the tender insides
of a sea anemone—
soft, red,

something to relish
for its fine, damp
texture.

Insects like them, too.
Once, driving Highway 99,
the morning

behind us in a hot glare of sunlight,
I bit into that moist
sweetness

opened my mouth and exhaled
a fog of fruit flies
creating

a kind of marvel, something
we'd laugh about for years,
my breath

casually born as tiny winged
creatures that longed
for nothing

short of what we all want:
to be fed,
enveloped.

CLIFF JUMPING

Once you're on top of the ledge
you can't crawl down
the canyon's steep face.
It's you alone, sharp stones
under your feet, the air's wide expanse
between your skin and the creek's deep pool
that shines like a windshield.

The dare is with yourself. Your friends
quit at twenty feet, a couple
at forty, everyone mindful of the kid
last May flown out by chopper,
spine snapped in a late-season swan dive.
Only a few each year claw their way
to the top scraggly outcrop
where a bad jump, any entry less
than soldier straight, can mean that placid pane
of silver breaks your arm or ankle
or neck.

Down below, girls sleek in bikinis
lie on their beach towels.
Their boyfriends plunge their arms
into a snowmelt eddy
for beer. Someone's brought a guitar,
its strumming far away—echoing
off the walls—as if imagined.

Then the shouting. Then the sunburned
faces all turned up to you
who wish it were over,

just past dusk, pickups and old Jeeps
bumping their way out of here
on Hog's Back Road,
carrying the brave safely off
the lava plateau.

You hear their voices and feel lighter,
as if the sun licking your back,
the little twig of star thistle
scraping your calf, touched
someone else. You are more alone
than the hawk that glides slow circles
in front of you.

COVERING THE CITRUS

At the back fence he leans the flashlight
against a clump of weeds,
points it through the dark at a sapling mandarin
barely up to his thigh, uses both hands
to unfurl an old blanket
over tender, waxy leaves. They'll burn
in even a light frost, he thinks,
those leaves like the skin
of a young girl, his daughter, say.
He can see her through the sliding door,
leaning over algebra equations,
her long dark hair hiding her papers.

The grass is wet. He points the light
at a young lemon,
covers it with a sheet. Already
he feels a snapping chill
through his jacket. His shoes
gasp in the damp soil. There is his wife
through the dining room window
paying bills. There is his daughter.
Here he is, protecting what he can
of the yard, wondering
how it would feel to be out all night,
how the cold sinks into the cells
and crystallizes. He thinks
of bed, being covered by a heavy blanket,
his wife's warm skin within reach.
Just how long could he stay
out here, how long before the cold
becomes a dull ache in his limbs,
before someone asks why he hasn't come in?

The Gardeners

The gardeners in the pickup ahead of me
laugh and sip their coffee.
In the back: two lawn mowers,
a weed whacker, a blower, a gas can.

I watch them joke about their wives
or replay last night's game,
waving their arms in the warm morning air
of the cab, comfortable in the moments

between their rushed talking,
at ease with the light—
neither summer nor autumn—
slanting through the gravel-pocked windshield.

They're glad to have each other
and the voice on the radio,
glad to be free of their monotonous beds,
to be heading into whatever landscape

they're hired to maintain. And I'm glad
to be in the sedan behind them,
on my way to work, eating buttered toast, imagining
the pleasant din of a mower, the smell of grass.

Puncturevine

Beware
its little thorn-studded seed casing
amid feathery leaves
in the driveway gravel
waiting
to pierce your bicycle tire
or the skin
of your instep.

Try to pull it up. Go ahead.
You'll succeed.
But next week they'll emerge—
small tendrils
from the taproot you snapped
underground.
You can spray
to wilt the leaves for a while
or just complain to your wife
as you show her
the drop of blood
on your heel.

Thrust your foot out.
Tell her
the blood is a symbol.
Tell her
something should be done
about invasive weeds
though you have no idea
what that might be
and feel good enough
hearing the pain in your own voice,
feeling the sharp ache
in your white throbbing foot.

One Lesson

If you fly a mile up
you'll see the rivers
like pliant twists of gleaming rope
dropped loosely over the valley.

Forget that.

Come down to the water's edge
where you'll feel the uneven
terrain of stones beneath your feet,
smell the green current,
hear traffic
rush behind you and a thicket
of willow and elderberry.

Take the hand
of your son or a neighbor kid
and walk with him into the river,
its icy life.

Tell him about the sturgeon
up from the Delta,
gut full of bottom life,
eyes pink beads of prehistoric
mystery. Tell him
that fish has been here
as long as his grandfather,
sliding around the bottom,
patient for something
we will never know.

Tell him to listen
to the lap and eddy of water,
to kingfisher—
whatever he can hear—
to sounds that make his pulse dance
and bring the world near.

AQUIFER

Under the heat-blistered walls of this house,
water laps and trickles between rocks.

It's dark down there—disturbed by no one—
just the occasional well like ours

sucking the liquid, gallon by gallon, up
through strata to sprinkler heads,

kitchen faucet, a tin cup
in my wife's hands, her lips. I want

an opening, a hatch in our back lawn
that hides a shining metal tube

we can slide down for hundreds of feet
until we splash in a room

of water, a cavern. My wife
would swim beside me, both of us

gliding through the pool
like otters, swimming, drinking, swimming,

gulping until we're under water
all the time, lifting our lips

to the surface to catch droplets
percolating out of the rock ceiling,

spilling toward our faces,
believers in a world that's gentle and cool.

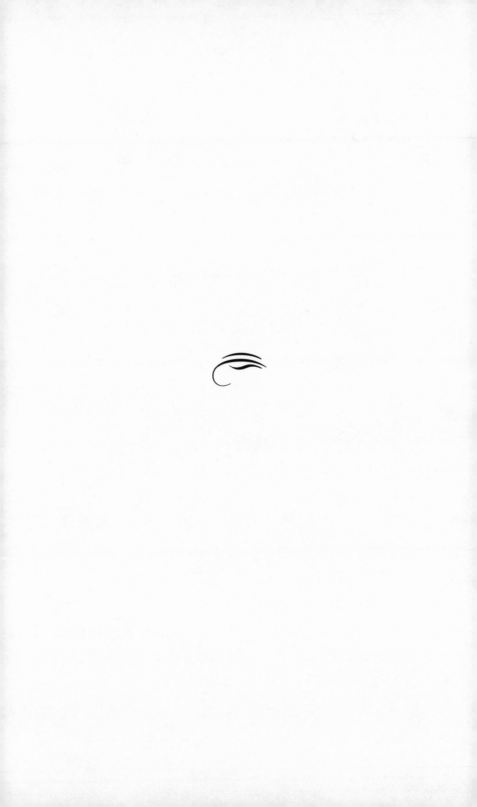

Eeling, North of Tomales

Up to my waist in kelpy brine,
a fizzing backwash at low tide,
I poke, jab, slide the eight-foot bamboo

pole through frothy surf
into pockets of quiet black water
under rocks. Here

the monkey-faced eels coil
their muscled bodies, hide
their smashed, dark faces.

God intended these creatures,
I suppose—jaws that can snap
fingers, tails flattened

into wide whips of power—
but hid them under boulders
encrusted with barnacles. I dangle

a chunk of squid
from eight inches of steel leader
and a heavy-gauge hook.

When one pulls, I pull back,
lifting it past anemones into air.
It twists, writhes

around itself, fights
the burlap sack I lower it into.
Today, a good day, I bag

three, plus a cabezon, carry them
a mile to the car. At home
on the back deck's redwood planks

I drive nails
through their heads
to quiet their still-flapping bodies,

then slice clean white fillets
from their bones and skin
which, under the porch light,

shines like wet leather, like
their own gleaming entrails,
something live and glistening within me.

On Making Wood

I took my job seriously, Dad—
to drag the brush away
through tall, hot grass
then build a pile for burning.
But I knew you
did the real work,
notching one side of a black oak,
then leaning the blade
and dangerous whirring chain
into the opposite bark
until it all roared down
in dust, leaves, and flying twigs.
You'd let the saw hang
at your side, idling,
your boots, hands, and arms
covered with snow
from inside the tree.

That dusting, in your hair, too,
and covering your pant legs,
was what I, at eleven, wanted.
I wanted to know how it felt
to be a man who had pulled greenchain,
a man who could stand with saw
in hand and not worry
about rattlers behind every rock. I wanted
to know which was harder, this
or lifting dead bodies off the snow
in Korea. Why didn't you talk more
of that? Why couldn't I know
how it felt to hear
bullets singing through the chill

around you, the muffled crying
voices of young men
whose last image of the world
was the sweat below your eyes?

I wanted you to talk to me, Dad,
to tell me again
how you spent your last shell
on a forkedhorn, had to wrestle
him by the antlers, cut his throat
while an old hunter on a hill
laughed at you. I wanted the whole
story of my great-grandfather
hanged and shot by Villa
and how your father, at fourteen,
buried him, then was forced
to dig him up and lay him down
on different land.

All I knew was the dust
of these stories, enough
to tell myself you started
kindergarten at seven, speaking
no English, that you would have worked
your life away in a saw mill
if not for the war, the GI bill,
the rancher's daughter you met
in college. All I knew
was that my arms were skinny
brown things, nearly useless
except for dragging off
what had already lived,
what was now trimmed,
and what would stay in a pile
until dry and lit with a match.

FROG EGGS

They started as a small slime
of black dots. After
wading through the pond
you and the boys,
sloshing a plastic bucket,
poured brackish water
into a clear bowl, and there
they were, a little jelly packet
of lives that grew daily
under our magnifying glass.
They're turning flat,
you tell me as you peer in
this afternoon, and I admit
I'm as caught up in this
as the boys who announce
any wiggle, any sign
of the tail, legs, gills.
But I'm content
to watch you watch the eggs, you
hovering over the bowl,
hair encircling your face
like dark ferns surrounding a pool
below a waterfall,
holding, accentuating the light.

Late Autumn, Late Afternoon

It's time to yank out the tomatoes—
overgrown, stems half black,
remaining fruit soft, inedible.

We do this together, cleaning up what is left
of acorn squash and tired peppers,
but I can't feel good about it.

The autumn wastes of a garden
are like half-formed thoughts,
dull and misshapen. One puny pumpkin

hangs on its withered tendril
in the field grass. I lob it
into the compost heap, watch it

roll against a moldy cucumber.
And you, hunched over the carcass
of an okra bush, could be a painting

by Millet,
but even that thought rots
into the damp soil at my feet.

Clouds press down in this ochre sky.
From across the pasture, our neighbor
sees us as faint shapes

moving against the horizon,
disappearing
right into the shadowed field.

Entering the Yard

Behind the house, where the redwood
planks of your deck
have long begun their soft rot,
you've placed a patio table
over the worst boards, those
that could swallow the ankle
of an elderly aunt or a grandchild.

This is where your daughter danced
at her wedding, where
your youngest opened
brightly-ribboned birthday gifts
a month before falling
like an angel or an oak leaf
into her grave.

It rained last night.
The May air, pungent with grass mulch
and roses, is like a prayer
for quiet. Tuberous begonias
stand alert with spiked dewy hairs
on their stems. You could nail in
new boards or watch

as morning sun
slants over the yard, a light
that covers the pool like foil,
circles tiny brown newts drowned
at the bottom, then climbs the hill
to the red and yellow freesias
opening their small mouths to the air.

About the Author

A native of northern California, Albert Garcia is the author of a book of poems, *Rainshadow* (Copper Beech Press), and of *Digging In: Literature for Developing Writers* (Prentice Hall). His poems have appeared in *Prairie Schooner, The Laurel Review, Poetry East, Mid-American Review, Yankee, The North American Review,* and other journals. Among his awards, he has received an Emerging Artist Fellowship from the Sacramento Metropolitan Arts Commission. Albert lives in the rural community of Wilton, California, with his wife, Terry, and three children and, after having taught community college English for 17 years, now serves as dean of the Language and Literature Division at Sacramento City College.